T0083349

IN WINDSOR FOREST

A Cantata for Mixed Voices

MUSIC ADAPTED FROM THE OPERA
SIR JOHN IN LOVE

R. VAUGHAN WILLIAMS

VOCAL SCORE

MUSIC DEPARTMENT
OXFORD
UNIVERSITY PRESS

NOTE

Orchestral Score and Parts may be hired

An arrangement of this Cantata, for S.S.A.,
is also published.

IN WINDSOR FOREST

No. I

THE CONSPIRACY

('Sigh no more, ladies')

(For women's voices)

Words by
SHAKESPEARE

Music adapted from the Opera
'SIR JOHN IN LOVE'
by R. VAUGHAN WILLIAMS

* May be sung by a solo voice if preferred.
Orchestral Score and Parts may be hired.

Copyright Oxford University Press 1931. Renewed in USA 1959.
Printed in Great Britain
OXFORD UNIVERSITY PRESS, MUSIC DEPARTMENT, GREAT CLARENDON STREET, OXFORD OX2 6DP
Photocopying this copyright material is ILLEGAL.

S. I
de - ceiv - ers ev - er,
S. II
de - ceiv - ers ev - er,
A.
- ceiv - ers ev - er,
A.
One foot in sea and one on shore, to one thing con - stant,
S. I
con-stant nev - er.
Then sigh not
S. II
con-stant nev - er.
Then sigh not
A.
nev - er.
Then sigh not so,
*Tutti from here

S. I
so. but let them go, Con -
S. II
so, but let them go, Con -
A.
but let them go, and be you blithe and bonny, Con -
B
p
f
-vert - ing all your sounds of woe in - to Hey hey, non-ny
pp

S. I
non-ny non-ny non-ny hey, hey non-ny
S. II
non-ny non-ny non-ny non-ny non-ny non-ny non-ny hey,
A.
non-ny non-ny non-ny non-ny non-ny non-ny non-ny hey,
S. I
non-ny non-ny non-ny non-ny non-ny non-ny non-ny
S. II
hey non-ny non-ny non-ny non-ny.
A.
hey non-ny non-ny non-ny non-ny.
p
f

C
S. I
S. II
A.
mf (Solo ad lib.)
Sing no more dit-ties, sing no mo, no mo
C
p
pp
p
D
So dull_ and hea-vy,
p
So dull_ and hea-vy,
mf
of dumps so dull___ and hea-vy
The
D
f

A.
fraud of man was ev - er so since Sum - mer first was
pp
S.I
First was lea - vy,
Then sigh not so
S.II
First was lea - vy,
Then sigh not so
A.
lea - vy
p (Tutti)
Then sigh not so
But let them
f
pp
S.I
but let them go,
Con - vert - ing all your
S.II
but let them go,
Con - vert - ing all your
A.
go and be you blithe and bonny
Con - vert - ing all your
f
pp

E
S.I
sounds of woe in - to Hey, hey non-ny non-ny non-ny non-ny
S.II
sounds of woe in - to Hey, hey non-ny non-ny non-ny non-ny
A.
sounds of woe in - to Hey, hey non-ny non-ny non-ny non-ny
E
f
S.I
Hey, hey non-ny non-ny nonny nonny Hey.
S.II
non-ny nonny nonny nonny hey, hey Hey.
A.
non-ny nonny nonny nonny hey, hey Hey.
fp
f dim.

F
Più lento
a tempo
S. I
Men were de - ceiv - ers ev - er.
S. II
Men were de - ceiv - ers ev - er.
A.
Men were de - ceiv - ers ev - er.
F
Più lento
a tempo
S. I
S. II
A.

No. 2
DRINKING SONG
('Back and side go bare')

(For men's voices)

Words by
JOHN STILL

Music adapted from the Opera
'SIR JOHN IN LOVE'
by R. VAUGHAN WILLIAMS

T. I
old.
Jol - ly good ale and
T. II
old.
Jol - ly good ale and old.
B. I
old.
Jol - ly good ale and
B. II
old.
Jol - ly good ale and old.
T. I
old.
T. II
old
B. I
B. II
B. I & II
I can-not eat but lit - tle meat, my stom - ach is not
as her life Lov-eth well good ale to
T. I
good.
seek.
T. II
good.
seek.
B. I
B. II
good; But sure I think that I can drink With him that wears a
seek, Full oft drinks she, till ye may see The tears run down her

T. I
hood
cheek
T. II
hood
cheek
B. I
B. II
hood. Though I go bare, take ye no care I am no - thing a -
cheek. Then doth she trowl to me the bowl, Ev'n as a malt - worm
cold
should
cold
should
cold; I stuff my skin so full with - in Of jol - ly good ale and
should; And saith 'sweet - heart, I've take my part Of this jol - ly good ale and
Jol-ly good ale and old
old.
old!
old.
old!
Jol-ly good ale and
pp cantabile

B. I
pp
Jol - ly good ale
p
and old,
B. II
old,
p
and old,
T. I
T. II
mf
I love no roast but a nut - brown toast, And a crab laid in the
Now let them drink, till they nod and wink, Ev - en as good fellows should
B. I
B. II
f
p
T. I
T. II
fire, A lit - tle bread shall do me stead, Much bread I no de -
do; They shall not miss to have the bliss Good ale doth bring men
pp
B. I
I love no roast, I love no roast but a nut - brown toast,
Now let them drink, now let them drink, till they nod and wink,

T. I
T. II
- sire. No frost nor snow, No wind, I trow, Can hurt me if I
to. And all poor souls that have scoured black bowls, Or have them lust - i - ly
B. I
And a crab laid in the
Ev - en as good fel - lows should
B. II
p
I love no roast, I love no roast but a nut - brown toast and a crab laid in the
Now let them drink, Now let them drink till they nod and wink, Ev - en as good fel - lows should
f
would, I am so wrapt, and through - ly lapt Of
trowled, God save the lives of them and their wives whe - ther
fire, I am so wrapt and through - ly lapt Of
do, God save the lives of them and their wives Whe - ther
fire, I am so wrapt and through - ly lapt Of
do, God save the lives of them and their wives Whe - ther
jol - ly good ale and old, jol - ly good ale, jol - ly good
they be young or old,
cresc.
jol - ly good ale and old, jol - ly good ale
they be young or old,
jol - ly good ale and old,
they be young or old,
jol - ly good ale and old,
they be young or old,
p cresc.

T. I
ff
ale
jol - ly good
T. II
ff
Back and side go bare, go bare, Both foot and hand go
B. I
B. II
ff
Back and side go bare, go bare, Both foot and hand go
ff marc.
T. I
ale and old, jol - ly good ale and
T. II
cold; But, bel - ly, God send thee good ale e -
B. I
B. II
cold; But, bel - ly, God send thee good ale e - nough, Whe - ther
T. I
old, jol - ly good ale and old.
T. II
- nough, jol - ly good ale and old, and old,
B. I
B. II
it be new or old, good ale and old, and

T. I
T. II
B. I
B. II
old
ff
1
mf
And Tib my wife, that
p
2
Presto
Jol - ly good ale and old.
Jol - ly good ale and old.
Jol - ly good ale and old.
2
Presto
ff
p
ff
ff

No. 3

FALSTAFF AND THE FAIRIES

(Round about in a fair ring-a)

Words by
SHAKESPEARE
RAVENSCROFT and LYLY

Music adapted from the Opera
'SIR JOHN IN LOVE'
by R. VAUGHAN WILLIAMS

S.
ring - a, thus we dance and thus we sing - a,
A.
T.
p
Trip and go, to and
B.
p
p
S.
mp
All a - bout, in and
A.
mp
T.
fro, o - ver this green - - - a,
B.

S.
out o - ver this green - - - - a, Round a
A.
T.
Round a - bout in a fair
B.
- bout in a fair ring - - - a.
ring - - - a.
dim.

A
p
S.
Round a - bout, in a fair ring - a, thus we dance and thus we
A.
Round a - bout, in a fair ring - a, thus we dance and thus we
T.
Round a - bout, in a fair ring - a, thus we dance and thus we
B.
Round a - bout, in a fair ring - a, thus we dance and thus we
f
S.
sing - a, Trip and go to and fro, ov - er this green - - -
A.
sing - a, Trip and go to and fro, ov - er this green - - -
T.
sing - a, Trip and go to and fro, ov - er this green - - -
B.
sing - a, Trip and go to and fro, ov - er this green - - -

B Adagio molto
S.
A.
T.
B.
- - a, all a - bout, in and out, ov - er this green - - - a.
B Adagio molto
ff
p
SOPRANO SOLO or a few voices (In free time)
Fair - ies black, grey, green and
pp
Oo
Oo
pp
Oo
Oo
pp
white
You moon-shine rev-el-lers and shades of

Alternative version when more than one voice are singing
of-fice and your qua - -
S.
night, You orphan heirs of fix - ed des-ti-ny, At-tend your office and your qua - -
S.
- - li - ty.
A.
oo
T. B.
oo
pp
C
Allegro vivace
A.
T. B.
C
Allegro vivace
f
p

ALTOS (a few voices)
A.
But till 'tis one o' clock, our dance of cus - tom round a - bout the
stacc.
A.
oak of Herne the hun-ter let us not for - get.
CHORUS S. and A.
S.
A.
But till 'tis one o'-clock, our dance of cus - tom round a - bout the
stacc.
S.
A.
oak of Herne the hun - ter let us not for - get.

SOPRANOS (a few voices)
Lock hand in hand,
f
p
stacc.
S.
your-selves in or-der set, and twen-ty
S.
glow-worms shall our lan-terns be to guide our measure round a-bout the
S.
tree.
ALTOS (TUTTI)
A.
A-bout, fairies, a-bout.
3
f
p

SOPRANOS (TUTTI)
S.
Lock hand in hand, yourselves in or-der set, and twen - ty glow-worms shall our lan - terns
stacc.
ALTOS
A-bout, fair-ies, a - bout. A -
S. A.
be to guide our measure round a-bout the tree. A -
TENORS and BASSES
T. B.
A-bout, fair-ies, a -
p dim.
S. A.
- bout, fair - ies, a - bout, a - bout.
T. B.
- bout.
dim.
pp

D Poco meno mosso
T.
B.
ff
But stay!
But stay!
D Poco meno mosso
ff
ff
I smell a man of mid - dle earth.
I smell a man of mid - dle earth.
p sub.
2
ff
Vile worm,
Vile worm,
ff
2
p

S. & A.
A
T.
— thou wast o'er - looked ev - en in thy birth.
B.
— thou wast o'er - looked ev - en in thy birth.
p
2
ff
S. & A.
tri - al, come.
T.
Cor - rupt, cor - rupt, and
B.
Cor - rupt, cor - rupt, and
2
p

S. & A.
A tri - al, come,
T.
taint-ed in de - sire!
Come, will this wood take
B.
taint-ed in de - sire!
Come, will this wood take
2
S. & A.
Come, will this wood take fire?
T.
fire, take fire?
B.
fire, take fire?
f
3
3

E
SOPRANO (Solo or a few voices)
A-bout him, fairies, sing a scorn - ful rhyme; and, as you sing,
f
Allegro
S.
pinch him to your time. —
SOPRANOS TUTTI
Pinch him pinch him black and blue,
A.
ALTOS TUTTI
Allegro
f
f
S.
Sau - cymor - tals must not view What the Queen of stars is do-ing, Nor pry in-to our fai - ry wooing
A.

S.
and pinch him black, let him not lack Sharp
A.
Pinch him blue,
let him not lack Sharp
T.
B.
S.
nails to pinch him blue and red, Till sleep has rocked his ad - dle head,
A
pp
T
Pinch him, fai ries, pinch him, fai - ries,
pp
B.

S.
Pinch him,
Pinch him,
A.
T.
Pinch him fai - ries, mu - tual - ly,
pinch him for his vil - lain - y.
B.

S.
A
Pinch him
and burn him,
pinch him
and burn him,
T.
B.

F
Presto
unis.
S.
A.
Pinch him and burn him and turn him a - bout, till can-dles and star-light and moon-shine be out,
unis.
T.
B.
F
Presto
ff
sim.

pinch him and burn him and turn him a - bout, till can-dles and star-light and moon-shine be out,

Pinch him and burn him and pinch him and burn him and turn him, till candles and starlight and moonshine be
Lento
S.
A.
gliss.
ff out.
T.
B.
gliss.
Lento
7
ff

No. 4

WEDDING CHORUS

(See the Chariot at hand)

Words by
BEN JONSON

Music adapted from the Opera
'SIR JOHN IN LOVE'
by R. VAUGHAN WILLIAMS

S.
ri - deth. Each that draws is a swan or a dove, and well the car Love
A.
ri - deth. Each that draws is a swan or a dove, and well the car Love
T.
ri - deth. Each is a swan or a dove, and well the car Love
B.
la - dy ri - deth, and well the car Love
S.
gui - deth; un - to her
A.
gui - deth; As she goes all hearts do du - ty un -
T.
gui - deth; un - to her
B.
gui - deth; As she goes all hearts do du - ty un -
p

S.
beau - ty; And en - a - moured do wish, so they might but en-
A.
to her beau-ty; And en - a - moured do wish, so they might but en-
T.
beau - ty; And en - a - moured do wish, so they might but en-
B.
to her beau-ty; And en - a - moured do wish, so they might but en-
f
p
cresc.
-joy such a sight, That they still were to run by her side through
-joy such a sight, That they still were to run through
-joy such a sight, That they still were to run through
-joy such a sight, That they still were to run through

S.
swords, through seas whi - ther she would ride
A.
swords, through seas whi - ther she would ride
T.
swords, through seas whi - ther she would ride
B.
swords, through seas whi - ther she would ride
f cantabile
A
p
Do but look on her
dim.
A
p

S.
A.
eyes, they do light all that Love's world com-pri - - seth.
T.
ppp
Do but look on her
B.
ppp
Do but look on her
S.
p
Do but look on her hair, it is bright as Love's star when it ri - - seth.
A.
T.
ppp
eyes, Do but look on her
B.
ppp
eyes, Do but look on her

S.
Do but mark, her fore-head's smoother than words
A.
ppp
Do but mark her, do but
T.
ppp
hair, Do but mark her, do but
B.
ppp
hair, Do but mark her, do but
S.
that soothe her; And from her arched brows such a grace sheds
A.
mark her,
T.
mark her,
B.
mark her,

S.
it - self through the face, as a - lone there tri-umphs to the
A.
ppp
Do but mark her
T.
ppp
Do but mark her
B.
ppp
Do but mark her
S.
f
life, All the gain, all the
A.
p
All the gain, all the good
T.
p
All the gain, all the good
B.
p
All the gain, all the good
p

B
cresc.
S.
good of the el - e-ments' strife.
A.
of the el - - - e-ments' strife.
T.
of the el - - - e-ments' strife.
B.
of the el' - - - e-ments' strife.
f
p
C
Have you
pp

S.
seen but a bright li-ly grow be-fore rude hands have touched it? Have you
A.
seen but a bright li-ly grow be-fore rude hands have touched it? Have you
T.
seen but a bright li-ly grow be-fore rude hands have touched it? Have you
B.
seen but a bright li - ly grow? Have you
marked but the fall of the snow be-fore the soil hath smutched it?
marked but the fall of the snow be-fore the soil hath smutched it? Have you
marked but the fall of the snow be-fore the soil hath smutched it?
marked the snow be-fore the soil hath smutched it? Have you
p

S.
or swan's down ev-er? Or have
A.
felt the wool of the beav - er or swan's down ev-er? Or have
T.
or swan's down ev-er? Or have
B.
felt the wool of the beav - er or swan's down ev-er? Or have
S.
smelt of the bud of the brier or the nard in the
A.
smelt of the bud of the brier or the nard in the
T.
smelt of the bud of the brier or the nard in the
B.
smelt of the bud of the brier or the nard in the

S.
A.
T.
B.
cresc.
fire? Or have tast-ed the bag of the bee? O so
D
f
white, O so soft, O so sweet is
f cantabile

S.
A.
T.
B.
pp
she
O so white,
p
fz
O so soft,
O so

S.
A.
T.
B.
sweet is she!
sweet is she!
sweet is she!
sweet is she!
ppp
pp
ppp

No. 5
EPILOGUE
(Whether men do laugh or weep)

Words from
Campion and Rossetter's Book of Airs

Music adapted from the Opera
'SIR JOHN IN LOVE'
by R. VAUGHAN WILLIAMS

T.
There is un - der - neath the sun no - thing in true ear - - -
B.
There is un - der - neath the sun no - thing in true ear - - -
p
A
S.
mf
There is un - der - neath the
A.
mf
There is un - der - neath the sun
T.
nest done,
mf
There is un - der -
B.
- - nest done,
mf
There is no - thing, there is
A
Voices

S.
sun, no - thing in true ear - - - - nest done, in true
A.
no - thing in true ear - nest
T.
- neath the sun, no - thing in true ear - - -
B.
no - thing un - der - neath the sun, in true ear - nest
B
f
ear - - - - - - - nest done, There
mf cresc.
done. Whe - ther men do laugh or weep, Whe - ther they do
- nest done. Whe - ther men do laugh or weep, Whe - ther they do
done. Whe - ther men do laugh or weep, Whe - ther they do
Orch. p

S.
is un - der - neath the sun no - thing in true
A.
wake or sleep, Whe - ther they die young or old,
T.
wake or sleep, Whe - ther they die young or old,
B.
wake or sleep, Whe - ther they die young or old,
S.I
ff
ear - - - - - - - - - nest, in
S.II
ff
ear - nest, no - thing in true ear - - nest, in
A.
ff
Whe - ther they feel heat or cold, There is un - der-neath the sun, no - thing in true
T.
ff
Whe - ther they feel heat or cold, There is un - der-neath the sun, no - thing in true
B.
ff
Whe - ther they feel heat or cold, There is un - der-neath the sun, no - thing in true
ff

C
S.I
true ear - nest done.
S.II
true ear - nest done.
A.
ear - - - - nest done.
T.
ear - - - - nest done.
B.
ear - - - - nest done.
C
ff
SOPRANOS
p
All our pride is but a jest.
p sub.
TENORS
p
None are worst and none are best.
p ALTOS
Grief and joy and hope and fear

S.
Vain o - pin - - ion
A.
play their pa - geants ev - 'ry - where, Vain o - pin -
T.
All
B.
Play their pa - geants ev - 'ry - where. Vain o - pin -
S. I
all doth sway, and the world And the
S. II
cresc.
all doth sway, and the world, the world is but a
A.
- ion all doth sway, and the world is but a play, is but a
T.
doth sway, and the world is but a play. Whe - ther men do
B.
- ion all doth sway, and the world is but a play. Whe - ther men do
D
ff
ff marc.

S.I
world is but a play, and the world is but a play, and
S.II
play, and the world is but a play, and the world, and
A.
play, and the world is but a play, and
T.
laugh or weep, Whe-ther they do wake or sleep, Whe-ther they die
B.
laugh or weep, Whe-ther they do wake or sleep, Whe-ther they die
S.I
the world, and the world,
S.II
the world, and the world,
A.
the world, and the world,
T.
young or old, Whe-ther they feel heat or cold, There is un-der-neath the
B.
young or old, Whe-ther they feel heat or cold, There is un-der-neath the

Halstan & Co. Ltd., Amersham, Bucks.

OXFORD UNIVERSITY PRESS